I0130006

LITTLE JUSTIN AND MOCHA-BEAR

THE TALE OF AN AMAZING DOG

JORGE A. CAMACHO

Copyright © 2025 by Jorge A. Camacho

All rights reserved. Except as permitted under the U.S. Copyright Act of 1976, no part of this publication may be reproduced, distributed, or transmitted in any form or by any means, or stored in a database or retrieval system, without the prior written permission of the publisher.

HIS Publishing Group
12426 Pleasant Valley Drive
Dallas, TX 75243

Printed in the United States of America
Hardback - 979-8-9926528-3-3
Soft Cover - 979-8-9926528-4-0
eBook - 979-8-9926528-5-7

HISPUBLISHING GROUP

Division of Human Improvement Specialists, LLC.
www.hispubg.com | info@hispubg.com

DEDICATION

I am dedicating this book to my precious Princess, Talyn Rose Camacho, my first granddaughter. She was born on November 3rd, 2023. She is incredible and an amazingly beautiful child. I love her so much. God Bless Justin and Trista Camacho, her beautiful parents.

SUNDAY MORNING

The year was 2003, and it was a beautiful Sunday morning. Little-Justin was riding his favorite toy, his bicycle, early in the morning on the neighborhood sidewalk, while his Father looked on. What a wonderful day for a bike ride; no school and no homework. They renamed the day Funday, and it quickly became little Justin's favorite day of the week.

He loved riding his bike, but like most boys at first, he kept falling. He kept trying, determined to get it right. He was getting close and knew that one day he would ride proudly through the neighborhood.

After several more Fundays, Little Justin finally accomplished his goal; he mastered the art of riding his bike. Seeing his son ride so well put a smile on his face. His Father proudly celebrated the occasion.

He wanted the very best for his one and only son. The most incredible feeling was knowing that Little Justin was making good decisions in life, in school, and was heading in the right direction. Little Justin also wanted to make his Father proud; he didn't ever want to let his Father down. The two of them had a beautiful bond.

One day after his bike ride, Little Justin headed home to get some rest. On the way, he heard a small puppy barking at him a short distance away from the side of a house.

Justin noticed how cute he was and wondered who owned him. Justin continued down the sidewalk, but the puppy continued barking. By this time, it was beginning to get dark, so he hurried the rest of the way home. He rushed in to tell his Father about the puppy. The two of them went back to see if they could find him.

THE LONELY ONE

When they got to the house, the little puppy started wagging his tail and was so happy to see little Justin. He asked his Father if he could take the puppy home.

His Father said, "No, I'm sure he belongs to someone nearby."

Little Justin lowered his head and said, "But he is all alone."

As they headed toward home, the cute little puppy kept barking as if to say, "Please take me with you."

The next day, Little Justin returned to see if the puppy was still there. He looked all over, but sadly, there was no sign of the puppy.

Little Justin thought to himself, "I bet something bad has happened." Not knowing what to do, he started walking back home. Suddenly, he heard a little barking sound. Sure enough, the puppy appeared, and he was so happy to see him. Little Justin was puzzled about why he was all alone; no one seemed to be caring for the cute little puppy.

He also wondered how in the world the puppy managed to survive. He longed to take him home, but he didn't want to disobey his wonderful Father. He respected his Father because of the love that his Father showed him.

That night, he worried about the puppy, afraid that something terrible might happen. So, the next day, he returned only to be disappointed. No puppy, no bark, and loneliness came over him. Little Justin felt miserable. He lowered his head and began walking home, wondering how the puppy had survived all those days without anyone caring for it.

Suddenly, he noticed something moving from off in the distance. In front of their house, the puppy was waiting for him and wagging his little tail. He couldn't believe what he was seeing. He thought, "How in the world did he get to their house?"

Little Justin quickly took him to the backyard so he wouldn't go into the street. He started to worry about how he would explain to his Father how this cute little puppy got to their home. He was afraid his Father wouldn't believe that the puppy had shown up all on his own. He didn't want to break their trust.

When his Father got home and saw the puppy, he gave little Justin a strange look. He said, "Son, we have to do the right thing and take the puppy back to that house. But I tell you what, this time we are going to find the owner."

Together they returned, but no one answered at the house. So, they knocked on all the neighbors' doors. No one knew anything about a little puppy. Confused how no one would have at least heard the puppy barking, they decided to put the puppy in the backyard. As the left they could hear the puppy barking in such a way it sounded like he was crying. Little Justin felt so sad.

Later that evening as it was becoming dark outside Little Justin and his Father sat down to eat dinner. They sat quietly eating, each thinking about the little puppy. Something didn't seem right. Looking outside their window little Justin knew that is was nighttime and wondered how the puppy was going to survive.

His Father went to the kitchen and on the way heard something at their front door. As he opened the door to his surprise there was a whimpering little puppy. He called to Justin saying, "Son, come to the door I think you need to see this." As soon as the puppy saw Little Justin his tail went wild wagging uncontrollably.

"Little Justin begged his Father, "Can we keep him? At least overnight. It is so dark outside, and he is obviously scared."

"I don't think we have a choice; this little guy is determined to be by your side." His Father said this knowing It would not be right returning the puppy at this hour.

Little Justin jumped up and down with joy. He wrapped his arms around his Father's neck and gave him a big hug. They he turned to the puppy and said, "Come on boy."

He ran to the kitchen and the puppy followed. He fed him some milk and some of their leftovers.

The cute little puppy drank all the milk and ate the food then looked up with those cute little eyes waiting for seconds.

His Father warmed up some more milk and pulled some leftover hamburger meat from the refrigerator. Little Justin got a bowl and filled it with water and set it by the back door. That was one of the best nights Little Justin could remember. The puppy snuggled up in bed, and they both fell fast asleep; exhausted by all the excitement.

The next day his Father said, "Justin, I still don't feel right about keeping the puppy without making another effort to find its owner." Sadly, Little Justin agreed and they returned to the house and knocked on the door once again.

Still no answer. So, they returned the puppy to the back yard of the house thinking maybe they worked odd hours. Wondering how the puppy had escaped they decided to act like they were leaving then they snuck around the side of the house and waited. Hoping to find out how the puppy was escaping.

They both laughed when they saw the cute little puppy digging at the fence. He dug a hole just big enough for him to escape. As soon as he got to the other side he ran toward their house.

This time they felt there was no other option but to keep the puppy and wait until someone came forward to claim it.

FINGERS CROSSED

Neither of them wanted to find the owner, but Little Justin's Father knew he would not be setting a good example if they didn't try harder to locate the rightful owner. He took little Justin back to the neighborhood and started knocking on doors asking if they knew anything about a cute little puppy.

Every time Little Justin's Father knocked on a door he crossed his fingers, hoping they wouldn't know anything. He knew in his heart that the puppy wanted to be his friend for life.

Two people were sitting on the porch at the last house they approached. When they asked them about an abandoned puppy, they told them that the people who lived in the house had packed up and left. They had been renting the house and the landlord told them they owed back rent and left many things behind.

They smiled at Justin and said, "Well young man I guess they left you a cute little puppy. Don't you think he deserves a good home with people who love him?"

Little Justin smiled from ear to ear. They were perfectly fit, a great match. The only thing lacking now was a good name for his new friend.

Since the cute little puppy looked like a small bear, he named it Bear. They hadn't thought about whether it was a girl or a boy until they saw it squat to pee. Little Justin and his Father let out a big laugh, and his Father said, "Well, son, I think you have a little sister."

Yes, it was a female, and they had given it a male's name. They continued laughing at their mistake. They had been so focused on locating the owner that they had paid no attention to whether the puppy was a boy or a girl.

MOCHA-BEAR

Father and Little Justin liked to visit a nearby Starbucks and order caramel mochas for each other.

They were standing in line waiting for their drinks when they both looked at each other and said, "Mocha!"

Little Justin said, "Let's call her Mocha-Bear."

That has been her name ever since. They had picked a beautiful name that they both loved for their precious family pet. Over time, she became more than a pet. Little Justin and Mocha-Bear played all the time; they were inseparable. If any other dog approached, she would protect Little Justin even if she was smaller than the other dog.

Six months had passed since he first found her, and she was growing fast. Every night she slept in his bed, and soon everyone knew that Mocha-bear was Little Justin's precious companion.

Every morning when Little Justin woke up, she would be right by his side. As he ate his breakfast, she was right there, always ready to protect him with her life. During the day, she would wander around the house, making sure there were no intruders. Mocha Bear was uniquely loyal and very smart.

When Little Justin returned from school, he began teaching her tricks. First, he taught her to sit and stay. Then he taught her to shake his hand and roll over. She was so smart and picked up every trick extremely fast. She loved it when the two of them went outside. She would run around the yard like a crazy dog but always kept an eye on Little Justin and wouldn't let strangers get close to him. Even the squirrels kept their distance as she chased them away.

BIRTHDAY WISHES

Time seemed to fly by as they played and lived life together.
Mocha-Bear was getting ready to turn one year old, and Little
Justin wanted to get her something special for her birthday.

He thought, since they had been introduced to each other on a Sunday
morning, that he would celebrate a funday for her as his Father had
for him. He designated May 30, 2003, as her birthday and funday.

Little Justin took her to the playground and threw a Frisbee
as far as he could, and Mocha-Bear immediately knew what to
do. She ran it down and caught it between her teeth in mid-
air and returned to drop the frisbee at his feet. She backed
up and sat looking at him with those excited eyes as if to
say, "Do it again." Which he did, time and time again.

Next, he hurled a baseball as hard as he could. The ball went flying, and Mocha-Bear took off after it. Little Justin laughed as she tried to grab the rolling ball with her teeth. Once secure, she ran as fast as she could and dropped the ball at his feet. They played for hours; she was so full of energy and loved playing with her precious owner. She was an amazing dog.

It had been a wonderful day for the two of them. Little Justin headed towards home, which was just a block away. As they rounded the corner and headed up the hill, a stranger approached, asking for directions, and Mocha-Bear quickly moved between Little Justin and the stranger, then started barking. The man, obviously, did not want any trouble, so he turned around and ran off in the opposite direction. For a female dog, she was bigger than most dogs twice her age.

Little Justin started first grade, and Mocha-Bear was almost two years old. Every morning, his Father would drop him off at school while Mocha-Bear watched. What a great pet she was, but more than that, she was his best friend.

When Little Justin was in school, Father would take Mocha-Bear to the store, go on daily walks, and feed her. She was very active and protective of him as well.

When he got out of school at 3:00 PM, his Father and Mocha-Bear were sitting next to each other waiting for him. She was always ready to protect them both. Mocha-Bear could sense trouble right away. It was in her blood, but most of all, she was loyal.

Mocha-Bear liked to wake Little Justin in the morning by licking his face. You could say that she was his built-in alarm clock. She also communicated using certain barks. Two straight barks meant she wanted to go outside to relieve herself. Four straight barks meant someone was outside, and Little Justin needed to be careful. When she ran in circles, it meant she was happy to see him, or she wanted to play.

Mocha-Bear liked to show happiness by standing on her two hind legs while Little Justin was on the couch. She would hug him with her two front paws. What a beautiful sight to see. Most days after an early dinner, Little Justin and Mocha-Bear would go to the school playground. He was allowed to go by himself, provided Mocha-Bear was with him. His Father knew what kind of pet she was. Mocha-Bear always stood tall next to Little Justin. She was brave and very protective. His Father knew what she would do if anyone tried to harm his son.

Mocha-Bear was a well-trained female German Shepherd. She was one of a kind.

LEFT BEHIND

While Little-Justin was in school, Mocha-Bear would roam
the house as if he had never left. When she realized he was
nowhere to be found, she would hunt down his scent.
Usually, she sniffed out the clothing that he owned or had worn.
However, sometimes she would find other items to play with.
One time, she picked up his scent on the television remote. Another
time, it was the remote control for the Game-Cube, one of Little Justin's
favorite games. That didn't go over too well. But as far as we were
concerned, Mocha-Bear was more important than any of that stuff.
Most of the time, she just jumped up and down with
joy, playing with his shoes and other items in his
room. Mocha-Bear could sure make a mess.

BAD GIRL

Little-Justin would come home from school and go into his room.
It was usually a total mess, and he would turn around and look
at Mocha-Bear and say, "Bad girl Mocha-Bear, bad girl!"
Mocha-Bear would pin her little ears down, which meant she was so
sorry. Little-Justin would just look at her, smile, and say, "Bad girl."
Then he would hug and pet her until she was back jumping up
and wagging her tail. He would tell her, "It's okay. It's okay."
Mocha-Bear would start licking his face with joy. Then she started
running in circles, which meant she was happy. Usually followed by
barking, which was her way of saying, "I want to go outside and play."
What a remarkable pet she was.

GUARDIAN ANGEL

Mocha-Bear was trained to walk without a leash. Usually,
we put one on her because of the city ordinance. You
could be fined if your dog were not wearing one. Father
liked taking her on walks, and they had a great bond.
But Mocha-Bear loved Little Justin with all her heart, maybe because
she felt he had saved her life when he rescued her. Little Justin
was the only one who had shown he cared. He was the one who
tried to convince his Father to do something when she was on the
other side of that fence. Mocha-Bear remembered everything.
She felt she owed him for that. What an incredible bond they
shared. Mocha-Bear was over three years old when Little Justin
was heading into the third grade. Every day when his Father
and Mocha-Bear dropped him off or came to pick him up, all the
kids would look at them. She would lick Little Justin on the face.
That was the love she showed to him, and all the kids knew it.

Some kids would laugh, others would show some kind
of generosity, and many would want to pet her.

After Little Justin went to school, Father and Mocha-Bear would walk
back home. When they came to an intersection or had to wait for cars
or buses to pass, Mocha-Bear would sit and wait like his guardian angel.
She wouldn't move until Father waved his hand, motioning her to go.

THE HOLIDAYS

It was December 2006; Christmas was approaching. It was just around the corner and would be here before we knew it.

Mocha-Bear would soon be four years old, and Little-Justin would be going into the fourth grade at the end of the following summer. Christmas came, and Mocha-Bear was spoiled. She got toys, balls, and more frisbees to play with. Little-Justin got many gifts from his family, neighbors, and, of course, his amazing Father.

But the most important gift of all was that he and Mocha-Bear had each other. They had become a family like no other, and their bond was awe-inspiring. Christmas was like a two-week vacation for Little-Justin. He didn't have to go back to school until after the first of the year.

With the New Year came fireworks. He would take Mocha-Bear outside, and they could hear all the fireworks going off. Many came from various fireworks displays around their neighborhood. But the best ones came from the Cotton Bowl. Little Justin and Mocha-Bear searched the sky in hopes of seeing the beautiful colors.

They played and kept an eye out until late in the evening.
When they heard the trembling sounds of the Boom…
Boom, they knew it was January 2007, a new year.

For them, it was a new beginning, and it was getting cold. It snowed
like crazy that February. Little-Justin and Mocha-Bear were able
to spend an extra week together because the schools were closed
due to the weather. Little Justin thought that was pretty cool since
he lived within walking distance of the school. Of course, many of
the teachers lived further away and couldn't drive on the streets.

He and Mocha-Bear enjoyed the time they
had together playing in the snow.

They stayed outside until late afternoon, when Father would call them to say dinner was ready. The two of them would dash to the house, knowing something good was waiting for them.

Mocha-Bear was raised inside mostly because Little Justin insisted. After all, she was an obedient and loyal dog. His Father agreed 100%. March and April flew by, and spring had sprung. On rainy days, Mocha-Bear and Little Justin would play in the rain, jumping in as many puddles as they could find.

TOGETHERNESS

May soon rounded the corner, and the weather seemed to be getting back to normal. Winter was now a distant memory, even though it had lingered well into spring. But they survived and even made it through the rainy season.

With Summer just a few weeks away, it meant that Little Justin and Mocha-Bear would be spending lots of time together. They could play outside and enjoy late nights. They would have movie nights on the weekends.

Little Justin got so excited thinking about all the fun they would have over the summer. He planned grand adventures for them. He was so proud to have such a remarkable pet, none like any of his friends.

Mocha-Bear was almost like having another sibling in the family.

They both communicated well, and he understood her regardless of her barking. Little Justin had adapted well to her language, and it was so incredible to understand each other.

Mocha-Bear liked taking baths, so whenever Little-Justin would say it's time for a bath, Mocha-Bear would go in circles and then run and jump in the bathtub. She loved the water and, at times, refused to get out. Little Justin would trick her by saying, "Let's play Ball Mocha-Bear." She would jump out of the tub, shake off the water, and head for the door.

Mocha-Bear was five years old, and Little-
Justin was going into the fifth grade.

The students at the school seemed to respect Little Justin more than
the prior year, maybe because he was in the fifth grade, or maybe
because his huge dog, which looked like a bear, was always by his side.

Little Justin had an influence on everyone at the school because
suddenly, everyone was asking their parents for a pet. You
guessed it, they all wanted a dog that looked like Mocha-Bear.

Little Justin knew there was only one Mocha-Bear, and no
one would ever find a dog like her. She always stood tall and
was very brave. Everyone knew she was protective of her
precious owner, Little Justin, and his Father. No one could
ever come between them; they had a bond like no other.

TESTING

The fifth grade seemed to fly by. It was towards the end of 2008, and all the students were required to take various tests. Little Justin passed every test, and his Father was so proud of him. His one and only son was smart, and he knew he had so much potential. He thought how lucky he was to have a son with such a bright future ahead of him.

Father worked with him on his homework and had to be patient. Mocha-Bear was precious and so special in many ways. She was also heading in the right direction and had a bright, long, and healthy life ahead. She excelled at every test they gave her. Fetching, protecting, behaving. She showed loyalty to both of them, especially Little-Justin.

SCHOOL'S OUT

No more homework. No more studying for Little-Justin. Nothing but fun, fun for both of them. School was fun, but getting to walk, run, and play together for hours on end was much more appealing. They had both earned it. Little Justin had passed every test, and his Father told him how proud he was of his performance in school.

They had a long summer to enjoy before Little Justin would be heading into his 6th and final year at the grade school. It was going to be a fun time for him and Mocha-Bear, and they planned to spend every minute together for the next two months.

THE ACCIDENT

One summer afternoon Little Justin and Mocha-Bear were playing with a beachball. It was an extremely windy day.

Mocha-Bear was always ready to protect Little Justin, no matter what. Little Justin continued to play with the ball, throwing it, and Mocha-Bear would run after it and managed to kick it back to him with her nose. She was incredibly talented.

Little Justin threw the ball up in the air again, but this time the wind blew, and it rolled towards the street. Mocha-Bear saw a car coming towards the ball. Little-Justin started running after the ball, but didn't see that the car was coming right at him.

As the car got closer. Little Justin realized it was too late to move out of the way. Mocha-Bear reacted fast and quickly flew towards Little Justin and pushed him off the street into the neighbor's front yard. Little Justin was safe, but Mocha-Bear was hit by the car.

Little Justin's Father was watching from a distance, and when he heard the screeching of the tires, he jumped off their front porch and started running towards Justin while screaming at the driver for going too fast. The driver hadn't seen Little Justin or his dog.

The driver could not avoid hitting Mocha-Bear. They were all amazed at how she had pushed her owner out of harm's way. The driver felt the impact and immediately stopped the car. He got out, began apologizing, and felt extremely bad.

Mocha-Bear was bleeding from her injury and was in obvious pain. Little Justin and his Father carefully picked her up and got her into their car. They rushed off toward the animal clinic, hoping their dog would be okay. She was losing lots of blood and needed serious attention.

Little Justin cried and cried, holding his precious pet. Mocha-Bear just continued to lick his face. Showing how much she loved him. She was a brave and loyal companion.

They arrived at the animal hospital and rushed her to the emergency area. After examining her the veterinarian said, "She has lost a lot of blood, so we will need to give her a blood transfusion."

Unfortunately, the clinic did not have her blood type, so they searched and searched for a clinic that could supply what they needed. Soon, they received a call from a clinic that said they had her blood type. They immediately ordered the blood specially for Mocha-Bear.

They informed Little Justin and his father that the blood would take between 6 and 10 hours to be delivered. A female veterinarian told them that the blood would arrive first thing the next morning and that they would perform the blood transfusion immediately. She assured them that Mocha-Bear would be fine.

Little-Justin and his Father headed home, planning to return early the next day. They arrived early, and Little Justin was still in tears, anxious to see his precious pet Mocha-Bear.

They waited and waited until finally the veterinarian came into the room where they were waiting patiently. She had teary eyes on her face, and Little-Justin knew something wasn't right.

He started crying while she broke the bad news. Mocha-Bear had passed away. She had developed an internal tumor, and it ruptured overnight.

The blood did arrive early, and they felt confident she was going to survive. But the impact from the accident had caused a small hairline cut on the tumor, which caused it to rupture. Everyone at the clinic was so kind, and they were all sad to see this unique, loyal, and intelligent creature go before her time.

Little Justin and his Father felt sick and were extremely emotional on that early morning. They were both quiet on the ride home. All Little Justin could think of was his Mocha-Bear. Things were never going to be the same for their little family.

He reflected on all the good times they shared, from the time he had first seen that lonely, cute little puppy at that house. He smiled, thinking of how she kept barking at him, wanting him to take her home. He remembered how she escaped from the yard and kept showing up at their doorstep. How they fed her warm milk, and she climbed into his bed and slept by his side. They were all good memories.

She had brought Little Justin Lots of love and joy that he had never experienced as a little boy. He was so thankful for all the amazing memories they both created and shared. Little Justin couldn't stop thinking that there should have been many more memories. He couldn't eat and fell into a deep sleep.

He started dreaming that he was playing with Mocha-Bear out in the middle of nowhere. It looked like they were in a big field with beautiful green grass. It was a beautiful day to be outside. Little Justin was throwing a frisbee, and Mocha-Bear would catch it in mid-air and bring it back, begging him to do it again, and again. The dream was so real that it felt amazing, awesome, and exciting.

They paused and took a break. Mocha-Bear was not communicating with her normal barking. She was talking to Little-Justin. It was an awesome experience for him.

She told Little Justin she left two puppies behind. They were in the back of the house, inside the garage, behind a tire. She added that one was a white puppy and the other looked like her.

The one that looked like a bear was a male puppy, and she told him to name it "Bear." She said to name the white female puppy "Alpha." What a fantastic dream it was.

Little Justin woke up and immediately went to the garage. He almost fainted at what he saw. The dream had come true. There were two precious puppies. He yelled at the top of his lungs for his Father. Who came running scared to death that something bad had happened.

Little Justin showed him the puppies. His Father stood there staring, not knowing what to think. Then Little Justin told him all about the most incredible dream he had ever experienced. He was so excited. He named them both with the names that Mocha-Bear had given him.

He would treat these two puppies so special. He would always feel Mocha Bear's presence. He knew that she was always nearby while he played with little Alpha and Bear.

THE END....

MOCHA

The Life of a Great German Shepherd
New book coming soon in 2026

www.ingramcontent.com/pod-product-compliance
Lightning Source LLC
Chambersburg PA
CBHW061223270326
41927CB00024B/3480